Here Today, Gone Tomorrow
How to Make Your New Year's Resolutions Finally Stick

Erin Bagwell, M.,A., Ed. S., LPC, NCC

Copyright © 2015 Erin Bagwell

All rights reserved.

No part of this book may be reproduced in any form without the written permission of the author, except in the case of brief quotations embodied in critical articles or reviews.

ISBN: 978-0-9915282-2-6

Published by Holon Publishing & Creative Community

Collective for authors, artists, and creative professionals - Holon exists to create symbiosis between artists of all kinds, businesses, non-profits, and their communities.

www.Holon.co

719 Virginia Ave.
Indianapolis, IN
46203

To learn about the author and her works, visit this book's website:

www.BagwellBooks.com

* * *

Printed in the United States of America

*For Tommy & my family,
who always believed.
Dedicated to the human race – may we always
be good to one another.*

About the Author
Erin Bagwell, M.A., Ed. S., LPC, NCC

Erin Bagwell is a Licensed Professional Counselor, and Nationally Certified Counselor, that has been a practicing psychotherapist since 2006.

Primarily, Erin provides psychotherapy for children, adolescents and adults at her practice in North Carolina. She helps individuals that experience depression and other mood disorders, anxiety, post traumatic stress disorder, phase of life problems, adjustment disorders, trauma related to abuse, attention deficit hyperactivity disorder, and many other problems.

Erin has always wanted to help as many people as possible, whether it is through psychotherapy in her office, spreading joy to strangers or simply through her writing. It is her hope that though you may not be able to spend individual time in sessions with her, that this book be a helpful tool for you to use in order to change your life.

www.erinbagwelltherapy.com

Table of Contents

Preface: The Dryer Trolls Took my Resolution	6
Too Much	10
Be Specific	20
Learn to Care for Yourself First	30
C'mon, Let's Be Realistic	38
Beware of Negativity	52
It's Not About What You Don't Want	62
Developing Your Reward System	68
Sharing Your Goals with Others	78
Flexibility Is Not Just For Muscles	84
Slow and Steady Wins the Race	93
The Bottom Line	100

Preface
The Dryer Trolls Took My Resolution

Happy New Year! Let me guess! You've already made your New Year's resolution? And this year you're really going to do it! Stop smoking. Lose weight. Get in shape. Save more money. Be a better friend. Stop stealing office supplies from work. Whatever it is, you are determined to keep *this* resolution. And I'm guessing you want some help with that, which is why you've decided to pick up this book. Well, I can't say that I blame you. I'm determined to keep my resolutions this year too.

You see, if you're like me, and countless others in this world, you probably set all of these wonderful idealistic goals every year and promise yourself that you are going to be the "best you" you can be this year. Nothing's going to stop you! The countdown ensues. The ball drops. You sing Auld Lang Syne…assuming you even know the words (I don't). And the party continues. You go to bed with the best of intentions, assuming you actually did *go* to bed and not pass out, either from pure exhaustion or intoxication… "Tomorrow I'll [fill in the blank]." But then something happens. Or maybe nothing happens…

For some of you it may happen as soon as the alarm goes off in the morning. You've vowed to get up and go for a run at dawn. It doesn't happen. The snooze button wins again. "I'm too tired today. I'll do it tomorrow." Perhaps, you have sworn off smoking, sweets, cheeseburgers, whatever it may be and you *try*! You give it everything you've got, which for some is more than others. Or maybe you come up with excuses that sound really good at the time. Regardless of what it is that stops you, you don't actually take any significant steps toward achieving your goal.

Then there are some of you who actually give that resolution a shot, and more likely than not, this is what I suspect has happened to you every year since you learned what a resolution was… A few weeks go by and during those few weeks you have time to gather rather impressive empirical evidence that changing yourself is much too difficult of a process and you

How to make your New Year's resolutions finally stick | Erin Bagwell

(through the scientific experimentation you have been conducting over the past few weeks) decide that you are perfectly content to remain exactly as you have been until some other external motivation arises that pushes you to become a better you. No, until then, you are quite satisfied to be the less-than-best you.

But what is it that happens to our best intentions? I believe that some of our good intentions simply disappear to the land of the lost socks. Don't make that face! You know exactly what *land* I'm talking about; and you know exactly what *socks* I'm talking about! The ones you swear you put in the dryer as a *pair*, but mysteriously that one sock emerges, all alone, eternally separated from its mate, sad and lonely. (I have some less than scientific evidence to suggest that really the dryer trolls are stealing the socks of the world to build some type of science-fiction ballistic sock weapon.)

So, in your life, do the dryer trolls come and steal away your New Year's resolution also? Do those nasty little dryer trolls steal your best intentions? No! Of course not! What would a dryer troll need with your best intentions!? Or your plan to become a "better you!?" Of course, dryer trolls have not been discovered by the ueber intelligent scientists who assign taxonomic rank to various species of beings, thus dryer trolls cannot be blamed; your sock has to be somewhere! And so does the "best you"!!

If the "best you" is out there, how do you find it? I know, I know. That's what you're supposed to be finding out. That's what you are hoping I can help you to find. But the answer must be prefaced by your understanding of why New Year's resolutions don't work for the majority of the population. If your New Year's resolutions never get lost in the land of lonely socks and you have never had a problem winning the War between the Treadmill and Pillow Topped Mattress, please use this book to fix the wobbly table in the break room at work. Or better yet, give it to that co-worker you know made a New Year's Resolution this year just like he or she does every year and passionately wants to achieve that resolution.

As a side note, I need to take a moment to discuss chronic patterns, or dysfunctional ways of living that have been present for many, many years.

As a psychotherapist, I see all types of people; people who are experiencing problems due to some significant change in their life (we call these phase of life problems or adjustment disorders), which are transient and expectable reactions to environmental stressors, as well as people who are "severely and persistently mentally ill."

More than likely the things that you are trying to change on your own are things that you *do* have power over and will be able to change with a little training and self-discipline. If on the other hand, you have picked this book up in hopes to change some chronic pattern in your relationships or your behaviors that would best be treated by a licensed psychotherapist or even by medication from a psychiatrist, let me encourage you to seek out more personal help and treatment than can be found within the confines of this book.

Even if that is you, keep hope! Severely and persistently does not mean "incurable." You have the power within yourself to cure anything from mental illness to terminal cancer! It's possible! Trust me, I have seen it and I know!

> "Incurable means curable from within."
> ~ Dr. John F. Demartini

For the rest of you, I hope this book will serve you in just the way that you need. I hope that it will be uplifting to you and encourage you to look within yourself to find the power to change those habits or patterns in your life that have been plaguing you for so long. You will get out of this book what you put into this book! So, give each of the steps 100% of your energy and you will find that 100% of your goals are achieved. You will be the person you want to be before you know it! And you'll have a great time on this journey! I believe it with all my heart!

Grab a pen or pencil and be prepared to use the application section of each chapter to reinforce the lessons covered in the text as well as to help prepare your plans for achieving those goals! Here we go!!

Sending you peace, love & happiness,

Chapter 1
Too Much

Sometimes the names of chapters can be misleading. I have tried to avoid that. The name of this chapter is the first mistake we make that causes us to be much less likely to succeed when we start trying to make changes. Two words: too much. In a nutshell that is the answer to your dilemma. You very well might be trying to change too much too quickly. Over the years, I have worked with clients experiencing an array of problems. And in my experience, I would venture to guess that if it weren't the beginning of a new year you probably wouldn't be feeling so obligated to make some changes, unless of course there is some less than desirable situation that has come up in life that now requires you to behave differently, such as an illness or major phase of life problem. So then, what is it about this *New Year* that makes us think that we have to change ourselves so dramatically overnight?

Let's look back to when and where this tradition of New Year's Resolutions started. One source reports that it was started by the early Babylonians who, wanting to begin each year with a clean slate returned all the farm equipment they borrowed over the previous year. Another source reports that it began around 153 B.C. when, Janus, the Roman mythical god of beginnings, came to represent resolutions, as he had two faces (so he could look to the past as well as to the future), and many Romans looked for forgiveness from their enemies and exchanged gifts before the beginning of each year. What I know for sure is that we all have been part of this tradition over the years and feel that January 1st is as good a time as any to make a change in our lives.

> Year's end is neither an end nor a beginning but a going on, with all the wisdom that experience can instill in us. ~Hal Borland

One of the most influential existential minds of our time, Victor Frankl, once said

When we are no longer able to change a situation, we are challenged to change ourselves.

I believe that once people come to the point in their lives when what they have done for so long is no longer working for them, they are forced to change. When the behavior that has served a purpose in the past, no longer serves that purpose we look at the behavior and re-evaluate, which typically leads us to an inclination of the necessity for change.

Now, change is a very difficult thing for any of us. No one likes changes. Not changes in their environments. Not changes in policies at work. Not changes in the world around us. Certainly not changes in something as personal as themselves. I understand this first hand, as most people do. Change is not brought about merely by the stroke of midnight. Change is a process; a very *difficult* process. Forcing change, especially when you are not ready for it, simply sets the stage for failure.

Well that just sounds negative, now doesn't it? How about instead of setting yourself up for failure, you set yourself up for success!? Doesn't that sound much more appealing? I thought so!

Imagine with me this scenario. Katie is a bright and promising young career woman who wants to make a few changes in he life. She resolves to arrive at work 15 minutes early, start running 2 miles every morning at 5:30 a.m., cut out sweets and caffeine, and start volunteering on the weekends at the homeless shelter. While those are excellent resolutions for Katie to have... that sounds a little bit too ambitious doesn't it? The desire to make this many changes in her life at one time is too much, too quickly. Talk about system overload! If you're like our friend Katie here, and have been setting between three and fifteen New Year's Resolutions every year, it's no wonder you feel like a failure. Sometimes one is a daunting task, but resolving to change this much at one time sends stress signals to your system eventually leading to that overwhelming feeling that "change is too hard," followed by the self-defeating thoughts like "I'll never change," or "I'm a failure." If this sounds like you, let me assure you that you are *not* a failure! You are an overloaded biological system.

> "Sometimes it seems your ever-increasing list of things to do can leave you feeling totally undone."
>
> ~Susan Mitchell and Catherine Christie,
> I'd Kill for a Cookie

Fortunately, just like on that old computer of yours that doesn't work as well as it once did, there is a reset button, and your system overload too is easily remedied. You didn't turn into the person you are today overnight and you cannot become the person you want to become overnight. Life is an evolving process. If you expect yourself to be able to accomplish this amount of change literally overnight, just because the ball dropped, and you made a lot of noise, you will be sorely disappointed. Which, I have a feeling, has happened to you at least once before or you probably wouldn't be spending this quality time with me right now.

The Fix

Start small. Set yourself up for *success*. Select one resolution at a time and resolve to give that all the energy you've got. It doesn't have to be limited to one resolution per year. You can have New Quarter Resolutions. Or New Month Resolutions. Or New Monday Resolutions (although I recommend maintaining your new changes for at least 14-21 days before trying to change something else, but I digress…more on that later). You don't have to wait until the New Year. Change one thing at a time and change it well, not just superficially. Every day is a good day to change!

> If you wait, all that happens is that you get older.
> ~Larry McMurtry, Some Can Whistle

How to make your New Year's resolutions finally stick | Erin Bagwell

I believe we have all heard it takes about twenty-one days to develop a habit. Where did that come from? Honestly… it was a plastic surgeon, Dr. Maxwell Maltz, to be exact, who recorded that he noticed that it took his patients on average of twenty-one days to learn to adjust to life without a recently amputated limb, and he therefore generalized that twenty-one day timeframe to include all major life changes. I have always felt that habits are so much more complicated than just a matter of "make it through the first twenty-one days and you'll be a different person."

For many years I felt like a failure after being able to stick with one of my resolutions for the first twenty-one days only to find that it held no actual permanence in my life after that. I thought I was the problem! If the whole world can change in twenty-one days, why shouldn't I be able to? Maybe even you have felt that way!

As a matter of fact, studies have shown that depending on the behavior that is trying to be established as the habit the range was anywhere from eighteen days to 254 days before the person felt as though that was part of their permanent identity, with the average being *sixty-six* days!!! Two-hundred and fifty four days! Ha! Twenty-one days my … well, you get the idea. And in case you were curious, here is some other information the researchers found: 1) Missing a single day did not reduce the chance of forming a habit, 2) A sub-group took much longer than the others to form their habits, perhaps suggesting some people are 'habit-resistant,' and 3) Other types of habits may well take much longer.

Patterns

Those habits that are more difficult to change, are the types of habits I lovingly (though there is not much to love about them sometimes) refer to as "patterns." Patterns are played out in our lives over years and years. Some people continue to find themselves in the same types of relationships with the same types of people over and over ad nauseam infinitum. This is a pattern that stems from a habit.

Patterns are much longer lasting and more difficult to change than habits. Habits tend to develop quickly and therefore can be changed more quickly, especially if one catches them soon enough. Those are the types of behaviors found in the study (such as drinking a glass of water every day) that felt more automatic after less than twenty days. Quickly formed, quickly changed. Little effort required changes.

Now, regarding patterns, I believe it takes three months to successfully develop a new pattern or change an old pattern. Research says sixty-six days. That is about three weeks less than three months, however the amount of determination and self-control that you invest into the change, the more successful you will become. The more permanence and automaticity you will experience. Pick one resolution and work on it 100% for three months. Then next quarter, make another resolution and continue the first one, thus "New Quarter Resolutions." At the end of one year's time, you will have changed four things about yourself.

If you have failed to feel a sense of permanency and automaticity in the three months, continue with the plan you are already using. Continue allowing yourself time to change until that new behavior becomes a part of who you are, which could be up to 254 days according to our brilliant researching friends.

Hopefully, by breaking down the changes into manageable sized pieces, and allowing yourself sufficient time to adapt to your new styles or behaviors, the changes in your life will be the larger, more significant things that you have been yearning to change for years.

> The field of consciousness is tiny.
> It accepts only one problem at a time.
> ~Antoine de Saint-Exupery

Application

What are four behaviors/patterns I have that I want to change about myself? What are the new patterns/behaviors you intend to replace those old patterns with?

Put the negative patterns in order of highest priority (most important to change) to lowest priority ("this can wait a few months").

1.

2.

3.

4.

Imagine next year at this time when you have changed these four things. How will life be different? How will you feel having changed these things?

How to make your New Year's resolutions finally stick | Erin Bagwell

{Notes}

{Notes}

Chapter 2
Be Specific

> "I don't care how much power, brilliance or energy you have, if you don't harness it and focus it on a specific target, and hold it there you're never going to accomplish as much as your ability warrants."
> ~Zig Ziglar

Often times when we begin setting goals they sound something like this: "I am going to lose weight." "I'm going to get in shape." "I am going to be more punctual." "I think I'm going to quit smoking." "I'm going to try to wake up earlier." "Maybe I'll blah, blah, blah…"

You may be thinking that those sound like wonderful resolutions. Perhaps you are recalling that you've said those very same things year after year. So what's the problem with goals or resolutions that sound like that? Simply put: the problem is that goals set in this manner are just not specific enough and they lack the language of commitment. It will be helpful for you to understand the reasons you feel the need to change and then plan how you will execute that change. Let's break this chapter down into two sections:

1. Your motivation, and
2. Your written plan.

> If you don't know where you are going, you will probably end up somewhere else.
> ~Lawrence J. Peter

Your Motivation

Any change is motivated by something and every desire to change is a natural thing to experience, although often times the actual process of change may be riddled with hardship and struggle. Some of these motivating forces are external, also known as extrinsic, and some are internal, or intrinsic. Think back to the times you or someone close to you has tried to change a child's behavior by offering them a reward when the child acts in the desired way. This is extrinsic motivation. They are getting something that comes from *outside* of themselves that makes them feel the behavior is worth the effort. That is simple enough.

Consider the caterpillar who is motivated to change into a butterfly – not because of peer pressure or because someone is going to give him a new video game, but because of some natural and internal motivating factor. Intrinsic motivation is often times infinitively more difficult for most people to find, and much more powerful once found. But it is this *internal* motivation that makes lasting change. I have never seen a butterfly turn back into a caterpillar! Have you? Then why do we revert back to our old selves, our old behaviors? It is because our motivation, the very foundation upon which we build our changes, is faulty. When the caterpillar changes, *he is changed*!

> "What the caterpillar calls the end of the world, the master calls the butterfly."
> ~Richard Bach

Now that you are aware of the two types of motivation out there, you have to figure out which one of those is going to be your beginning force (what is going to get you started) and which will be your sustaining force (which is going to keep you going when you don't feel like you are compelled by the outward rewards anymore). Many times, the external factors help get us started but the internal factors are the ones that will keep us going. If you do not spend sufficient time determining those internal, or intrinsic factors that motivate your change, you will find that the momentum fizzles out and your journey will stop.

For instance, consider the person that wants to lose weight. They may have the following external motivators: 1) fit into a size eight and 2) Look good in a bikini. The external motivators may have enough power to start their journey and the external reinforcements they receive (the compliments from others noticing their weight loss) may have enough juice to sustain them briefly but, let's face it, those are just not the right reasons to embark on such a difficult journey. That would be like Ferdinand Magellan and his crew saying "we're going to sail around the world because I want this hot chick to like me." Ridiculous. Magellan died during that journey. If he had not been motivated by that internal "I have to have it" force he would never have set sail. I am not downplaying the importance of external factors; I am simply saying that they are not the most significant when people begin on potentially long journeys to make long term changes.

More appropriate motivating factors are the intrinsic ones; the reasons you have to change that are just for *you* and no one else. Perhaps reasons like "I want to live a long life to meet my great grandchildren," or "I am worth spending 30 minutes a day on myself." These are the motivations that will help you push through the urge to quit, which is going to happen. These are the motivators that are going to inspire you when you have lost inspiration from the world. These are the motivators that are going to help you become the self-disciplined person who does reach those goals. And discipline is a very important part of it… just having the beliefs is not enough. We'll talk more about that later.

> Success isn't a result of spontaneous combustion.
> You must set yourself on fire.
> ~Arnold H. Glasow

Your Written Plan

Although we as human beings are capable of having abstract thoughts, results are not produced simply out of abstract ideas. Unfortunately the "want to" is not enough to get it done. Those ideas must have a specific action plan in order to produce results. We cannot work towards an abstract idea and see measurable results. The human brain works best when we

How to make your New Year's resolutions finally stick | Erin Bagwell

specifically assign it a task to complete.

Prior to my work as a psychotherapist, I was providing case management services for individuals with intellectual and developmental disabilities. Part of my job was to sit down with their "treatment team" (a team of people who assembled to help determine how to best serve the individual) and develop a plan that would help them achieve their life goals. Since the services provided to these individuals were funded by the state, it was very important that these plans for how they were going to accomplish their goals be very specific and measurable. The state needed to collect data that the individuals were in fact making progress to justify paying for the services for another year. After using this method to help others reach their goals for years, I realized one day that this method may also work in the personal lives of individuals who had not been diagnosed with intellectual or developmental disabilities. Through this realization the idea for this book was born.

So, what is it that you really want? Specifically!? Do you want to lose twenty, thirty, forty-two, or 56.8 pounds? Do you want to go down two pants sizes? Do you want twenty-five inch biceps? Do you want to be five minutes early ever where you go? Do you want to smoke three less cigarettes per day?

In order to successfully accomplish a goal, we must first successfully set the goal. And that means we must hold in our minds exactly what it is that we want. But holding it in your mind is not enough. You need to commit to paper a written plan of what the long term goal is, as well as the smaller steps you will take in order to accomplish it. Writing goals and plans to accomplish those goals helps bring a deeper sense of contract with, commitment to yourself and commitment to your goals. When writing the goals, however, you must write them in very specific terms, using very specific time frames.

Time frames are important because they give us that measurable amount of time in which to accomplish our goals. The difference between a dream and a goal is a time frame. On the calendar, that date gets closer and closer, each day you wake up. Each day you can look at the date and measure your progress against that time frame. If you are successful in setting the goal, meaning your goal is supported by a very easy-to-follow action plan, designed by you, then seeing progress on reaching your goal should encourage you to keep pushing towards its total accomplishment. The simple act of accomplishing a goal is often helpful in motivating us to continue setting new goals. Each successful attempt results in a desire to develop new goals and keep reaching them, one after another. With each step you are becoming the "best you" you can be!

> Make the most of yourself,
> for that is all there is of you.
> ~Ralph Waldo Emerson

Within each and every one of us exists a part that wants to experience that satisfaction of success. The very act of selecting a target date to achieve the goal will either drive us ("oh, the target date is coming up, I better do my best") or provoke an intense anxiety within us ("oh, the target date is coming up, I can't do it, I might as well just quit while I'm ahead").

Now if you are one of those who tends to have anxiety when you realize that you are getting close to the target date and haven't made as much progress as you would like… as in, your 25 year high school reunion is coming up in one month and you have only lost four of the twenty pounds you wanted to lose… *DO NOT GIVE UP*! Change your way of thinking and the results will come!

But first let's look at your motivation and get a plan started to help you accomplish those goals.

> "Success isn't the key to happiness;
> happiness is the key to success."
> ~Albert Schweitzer (1875 - 1965)

Application

Why do you want to make this change?

What are your external motivators?

What are your internal motivators?

What will keep you going when you forget your reasons?

How to make your New Year's resolutions finally stick | Erin Bagwell

Use the same format of the table below to record the specifics of your goal(s):

(P.S. – try to keep the changes for the first 7 days of the cycle to no more than 3 – more than 3 will make the changes harder to stick with…)

Specific Goal with Measurable Results	Changes for the 1st 7 Days of the Cycle:	Changes for the 2nd 7 Days of the Cycle:
I will lose 10 pounds in 5 weeks.	I will reduce my intake of processed sugar from 7 times per week to 4 times per week for the 1st 7 days. I will walk for 20 minutes on Monday, Wednesday and Sunday this week. I will replace two of my daily beverages with an 8 ounce glass of water.	I will reduce my intake of processed sugar from 4 times per week to 3 times per week for the 2nd 7 days. I will walk for 25 minutes on Monday, Wednesday and Sunday this week. I will replace 3 of my daily beverages with an 8 ounce glass of water.

{Notes}

{Notes}

Chapter 3
Learn to Care for Yourself First

When setting your goals it is very important that you are realistic in your desired outcome. First and foremost, it is important for you to sit down and think long and hard about what it is that you want to achieve. Be absolutely sure that these goals are what *you* want and not what anyone else in your life, including your family or your friends, wants for you. Much less, setting goals based on what society dictates is acceptable regarding your behaviors or appearances! Hopefully, the exercise in Chapter 2 helped you begin that process.

This precious life is yours. It does not belong to anyone else and you must live it for yourself! Sound selfish? I don't care. Sometimes being a little selfish is a good thing, especially if it helps you become a better *you*. You cannot care for other people, including your children, family, friends, strangers, etc., if you do not first have your emotional cup full of goodness, happiness and peace.

> Be there for others, but never leave yourself behind.
> ~Dodinsky

I suspect that if you were already as full of goodness, happiness, and peace that you longed for you would not feel the urge to change anything, and thus would not be reading these words right now. That means that *you* above all other people need to be hearing what I am saying! *You are very important and worth caring for in the best way you know how!* Maybe you don't know exactly how to care for yourself at this point. The lessons in this book will help you begin to care for yourself in an appropriate way, and in the way that you deserve.

Many times we get so caught up in caring for others that we forget to care for ourselves. Maybe we don't "forget," more than likely we are making a conscious effort to neglect our own wellbeing. We say "I need to exercise but my family needs me to wash the clothes," or "I want to sit down and read a good book, but my friends need me to help them with a benefit for the elderly." *Are you kidding me?!* They may *want* you to do those things really, really badly – but they don't *need you to be the one that does them.*

Teach an older child how to wash clothes, ask your significant other to wash a load if they need to be done that badly. Tell that friend of yours who always wants you to help them with things (but seldom helps you with things in return) "no." You don't have to be rude to them about it but you do need to learn to say "no," especially when it involves caring for others as your top priority, when in fact it is *you* that desperately needs to be cared for yourself.

Some of you may feel guilty for taking time out or away from your responsibilities to care for yourself. I know many people have experienced these feelings, including myself. You want to take that time to do something you enjoy or something that is good for your emotional, physical or spiritual health, but you feel guilty because you have other obligations that need to be addressed first. But I am telling you today that it is alright to take care of yourself. Your family wants you to be happy and they will understand if you need a little time to do something for yourself. It may be a little difficult for them to adjust to you being gone thirty minutes a day or an hour a day so that you can do what it is you need to do, but they *will* adjust and they will be grateful for the new, improved, happier, and more peaceful version of you they get in return.

> To free us from the expectations of others, to give us back to ourselves - there lies the great, singular power of self-respect.
> ~Joan Didion

Be a little selfish. If you need permission, I am giving it to you right now! I don't mind being the bad guy. Tell your family and friends that "Erin said it is my homework to take time for myself." (Of course, they are probably going to ask you "who is Erin!?" Well, you just pay that question no never mind and go about the business of *caring for yourself*. Put off doing something that others want you to do so that you can be disciplined enough to accomplish what *you want to do*! Sometimes this means saying "no" to others for a little while so that you can learn to care for yourself again. There are many things you can do that will help you learn the pattern of regularly caring for your emotional, physical or spiritual wellbeing. In the application section, I have included a sample list of recommendations for how you can begin to engage in regular self-care. This will assist you in evaluating and further developing those patterns in your life.

Application

Review the following recommendations as suggested by James Guy and John Norcross and then make changes in your life where you see that changes are needed.

1. Evaluate the quality of your sleep, your nutrition. Do you get sufficient exercise and healthy food during the day or are you surviving on diet soda and pretzels to sustain your energy?

2. Increase the amount of sensory awareness you engage in – notice your surroundings using all of your senses (vision, touch, hearing, gestation and olfaction) and enjoy the wonderful things the world has to offer you – the smell of a rose, the taste of good food, the sight of a beautiful sunset – and give gratitude for each of those.

3. How is your sense of humor? This can do a lot to reduce stress in your life.

4. Exercise and relax regularly.

5. Take a small break to self-massage your face and neck muscles. Schedule a regular full length massage to nourish yourself and relieve tension in your muscles.

6. Routinely engage in a hobby – reading, taking vacations or mini-breaks, attend artistic events and movies. Is your life really balanced?

7. Pace yourself. Everyone needs some down time. Schedule breaks for yourself and actually take them.

8. Is play a staple of your emotional diet? We all need to have time to be a kid again. Climb a tree (I just did this recently and it was super fun), play in the rain.

9. Enhance your environment – get more comfortable furniture, aesthetics in your décor, nourishing food in your refrigerator, etc.

10. Reassure yourself that the conditions in life are not always easy. This is unfortunate but not the end of the world.

11. Assertively lessen unrealistic demands made on you: don't take on more work than necessary or wrongly believe you're expected to do more.

12. Catch yourself when you begin to believe that you are the cause of negative circumstances in the lives of others. Self-depreciation is self-defeating! Consider alternate explanations that may cause events.

13. Can you identify and resonate to an abiding mission or spirituality for your life – this tends to bring a higher satisfaction in people.

14. How does your belief in a mission, God or a transcendent force serve as a resource for you? Sometimes we have lost ourselves and lost our sense of meaning and purpose. Have you lost yours? Is it time to find it again or reevaluate your current spirituality or lack thereof?

What are some other changes you could make of that will help you care for yourself better and on a more regular basis?

What are some activities that you are currently doing that you could replace with caring for yourself?

How to make your New Year's resolutions finally stick | Erin Bagwell

{Notes}

{Notes}

Chapter 4
C'mon, Let's Be Realistic

Being realistic when setting your goals means that there may be barriers or obstacles, either physical in nature or otherwise, to achieving your goals. Whether it is achieving your ideal body image, weight or some other type of physical transformation, you still must be realistic. (I am going to use this example because it is the most common goal in our country currently and has been for the last decade, if not more.) For instance, it is ridiculous to believe that I, at five feet, seven inches in height will be able to survive at a weight of 103 pounds. That is not realistic for my body type, not to mention attempting it would be physically damaging to my body. In order to be realistic when setting your goals, you must focus on three areas in order to be successful: 1) setting measurable goals that occur in stages, 2) realizing potential obstacles, and 3) knowing your triggers.

Setting Measurable Goals

Measureable goals are ones that help you track your progress. This is different than the plan to achieve the goals. Measurable simply means the guidelines by which you are able to objectively evaluate your progress. They are more scientific, or logical, in nature. Your measureable goals should be developed and tracked in a way that when complete you would be able to make a chart or a graph out of the data you have gathered and present them at your eighth grade science fair all over again!

Take a man with a large frame who is six feet, four inches tall who would like to reduce his weight from 280 pounds to what would medically be his "ideal body weight." According to the charts that range would be from 181 pounds to 207 pounds.

The larger goal would state: I am going to lose 73 pounds, in 40 weeks (see how he is being specific about a time frame!). The smaller, measurable goals should be set in stages. First, he may set his first stage goal as losing eight pounds by the end of the month (which stays with his original time frame) and once that is achieved he gives himself a reward. The subsequent stages may be set based on a timeframe (one month, one week, etc.) or how many times he wants to perform a certain behavior in a given time frame (i.e. work out three times per week for forty-five minutes).

Once he has reached his overall goal of losing 73 pounds, the next part of the staging involves seeing how living at that recommended weight feels, he may evaluate to see if another stage needs to be added to his goals, because it is possible that his lifestyle does not allow him to live reasonably at the lower end of his "ideal weight." If it is determined that ideal weight suits his lifestyle well, then he should strive to be the fittest person at that weight on the planet. As a side note to everyone, like I said in Chapter 3: Do *not* try to *starve* yourself to fit into any preconceived ideas of what beauty or physical attractiveness is, especially as dictated by today's airbrushed society.

Some of you may have goals that have absolutely nothing to do with weight loss or improving your physical body. But just because your goal has nothing to do with getting thinner or fitter does not mean that you don't have to be realistic too. You may have a goal to change the world, it is unlikely, however, that you will run for president in order to change the world. But you can change your goal from such a generalized perception to one that sounds like this: "It is my goal to make one person happier today by spreading my happiness through smile or song." This sounds pretty realistic to me! You may not change the world, but you can change the world for somebody.

That reminds me of the story of a man who walked up and down the beach with his grandson. His grandson picked up one starfish at a time and tossed it back into the ocean. The man, who had become hardened and cynical in today's world, said to his grandson, "Son, why are you bothering? You cannot possibly throw all the starfish back into the water. You're not making any difference at all." The grandson replied, as he tossed another starfish back into the water, "It made a difference to *that* one."

Societal Demands

> It is no measure of health to be well adjusted to a profoundly sick society.
> ~Krishnamurti

Let me take a moment to say one more important thing: Many times we are setting goals because we feel the need to change things in our lives because other people are (or society, in general, is) telling us that we need to be a certain way to have approval or to be loved or accepted. We have a record playing in our minds, or a playlist on repeat, saying "you should be more generous," "you should be skinnier," "you should be blah blah blah…" And we tend to believe these messages because they also come with the idea that by achieving these societal demands placed on us by others we will be deserving of their approval, acceptance, or love. This is a lie! If there are people in your life that require you to earn their love, they are not giving you true love at all, regardless of whether they are your family, significant others or friends. Love in its purest form does not have to do with whether or not someone meets the qualifications! Hear this, now: *YOU DESERVE TO LOVE AND BE LOVED!* Understand also that you cannot give love without first loving yourself. This is why it is very important to care for yourself, as I discussed in the previous chapter, and why it is important for you to set goals and achieve them because those goals are things *you* want to accomplish in life.

> "The finest clothing made is a person's own skin, but, of course, society demands something more than this."
> ~ Mark Twain

Realizing Potential Obstacles

As with any race you run, when setting your goals, there will be obstacles. And at different times there will be different obstacles, though

How to make your New Year's resolutions finally stick | Erin Bagwell

you may be running the same race.

I call myself a "runner." I run. Not very quickly, but I run. When I first started running, I trained and began completing a few "official" 5k events (meaning I got t-shirts for my participation!!). The first 5k I ran was a breeze! I thought, "Wow! I could do this every day!" The second of which had many more obstacles than the first (for one, I was running in a brand new pair of shoes because I forgot to pack the ones I already had broken in) and was more difficult. But… there is one 5k that stands out to me as a *beast*! We were running through raging creeks, fields of high grass, mud, across jagged rocks, up steep embankments… just beastly! It was very different from the first few races I had run.

I had no idea before I started that this race that it was going to be full of obstacles like those, except that my sister-in-law (who had run that very course several times before) said to me, "this is a very slow course." I thought "Um, all my courses are slow…" Obviously as a new runner I didn't know that meant it was slow because it was full of obstacles that would slow anyone down. Boy was it slow, or was I slow, I should say! Same distance, three times. All with different obstacles. All with different results.

For each goal we set there will be obstacles. Those obstacles will be changing depending on the person and the time in our lives that we are setting out to accomplish this particular goal. Knowing your obstacles in advance will prevent some of the side effects (so to speak) of running unprepared.

How does this apply to you, assuming that running is not your goal? Well, you first need to know what types of obstacles there are when accomplishing goals. I will be talking about two types of obstacles:

1. Physical; and
2. Mental/emotional.

Physical obstacles

Physical obstacles can be things related to your physical health, but also include things like financial limitations, time constraints, and your general environment.

The most common physical obstacle that people complain about is a lack of time. "I don't have time to go to the gym," or "I don't have time to take time for myself." The key here is not to continue with those types of statements but to really and honestly evaluate what you are spending your time on. Are you wasting time redoing things that you are not doing right the first time around? Are you watching hours of television each day? Or perhaps, you are addicted to Facebook games or social media? Don't even get me started on how much time social media takes from our days.

When you are setting goals and working towards the ideal self, you will need to sit down and realistically look at what you spend your time on. Are these activities enriching your life? Are they helping you achieve your goals or are they hindering you? I don't know of anyone who has achieved their goal by watching hours of television, unless of course their goal was to break the record for the most consecutive hours watched. As a general rule, I limit myself to about an hour per day of television (with the exception of NFL Sunday during football season). I love my DVR – by recording my favorite shows, I eliminate the wasted time watching advertisements and can use my hour of television watching more productively. This allows me to use my other time more productively.

For other physical obstacles, like financial ones, sit down before starting the goal and figure out what you will need to achieve the goal. How much will it cost? How much time do I need to invest? What is my time worth monetarily? What other resources may I need (i.e. a gym membership, exercise equipment, CDs, DVDs, a babysitter, a cleaning service, etc.)? And from there you can have a clear idea of the time commitment and other resources it will take to achieve your goal.

> "Most people have no idea of the giant capacity we can immediately command when we focus all of our resources on mastering one single area of our lives."
> ~Tony Robbins

Mental/Emotional Obstacles

It is very important that you understand you're your emotions are directly connected to your thoughts. You cannot be thinking good thoughts and feeling bad; conversely you cannot be thinking bad thoughts and feeling good. Your emotions reflect your innermost thoughts, conscious or unconscious, and so it is very important to be aware of how your thoughts can then become obstacles on your path to reaching your goal.

Mental, or emotional, obstacles can rear their nasty heads in many different forms, the majority of which are what has been referred to as "stinking thinking." These thoughts bombard us when our emotional cup is not full enough. Thoughts like "I'm not good enough," or "I always fail." It is part of the human condition. Human beings have struggled with low self-esteem since the beginning. Some of the earliest evidence of low self-esteem is learned in the Christian and Muslim stories of Cain killing his brother, Abel, because of his feelings of jealousy. Jealous feelings always come from a root of insecurity or low self-esteem.

Be prepared for these thoughts to make their way into your life as you begin to make these changes and in preparation think of what thoughts you are going to use to replace this stinking thinking. Instead of "I'm not good enough," think "I am successful at every aspect of my life." Instead of "I never do anything right," think "I give it my all and success follows me where ever I go!" Part of success is the ability to *think* your way to success! Unfortunately, we also think ourselves to failure.

> "Whether you think you can or you can't, either way you are right."
> ~Henry Ford

There are many different types of stinking thinking but here are just a few. Use this chart to help you rewrite the script with that stinking thinking you have once and for all:

Stinking Thinking	New Positive Thought
I will never reach my goal.	I am getting closer to my goal every day!
I don't have enough money to reach my goal.	Money comes easily and frequently!
I've already tried that and it didn't work.	I learned from my last attempt and this one will be more successful!
I am no good at this.	I am successful at everything I attempt!
I am too tired to work on me.	I have more than enough energy to do all I want to each day!

"The words 'I am' are potent words; be careful what you hitch them to. The thing you're claiming has a way of reaching back and claiming you."
~A.L. Kitselman

Another form of mental obstacle may have to do with an inability to concentrate or focus. Lack of focus can be attributed to many things, but I have discovered the most frequently occurring cause is simply exhaustion. This is happening more and more in today's world. People get so burnt out on everything else in life that they don't have time for the important things. Get plenty of rest. Do nice things for yourself. Fill up your emotional cup so that your brain can be an ally on your journey, and not an obstacle in your way.

> Men are not prisoners of fate,
> but prisoners of their own minds.
> ~Franklin D. Roosevelt

Knowing Your Trigger

Triggers refer to the types of situations or circumstances that get you derailed from the course you have laid out for yourself. They are similar to obstacles in that they will arise and create a situation that you must choose to overcome and persevere, or you must choose to quit. Triggers are most likely deep rooted and will cause emotional responses which are often unconscious, meaning that you react before you are aware of your reactions.

For example, if you have heard messages since childhood that resulted in perceptions that you are not good enough, a negative word or criticism will likely discourage you or push you toward inaction more easily than it would if you had not been fighting with these types of feelings for many years. It is also possible that these emotional triggers may be causing the problem in the first place, as a way of coping with the negative emotions that have been created. For instance, you may be binge eating to feel full when you feel emotionally empty. Without identifying the root of the emotional issue causing the behavior, changing the behavior will likely fail. If you are not able to cope with the negative feelings in a more positive way, the dysfunctional coping skills will not be released.

Triggers can also refer to something that happens immediately before the behavior you are trying to change usually occurs. For people who may want to stop drinking or smoking, the trigger may be a meal (since you most likely smoke or have a drink after eating), or the end of a long day at the office. Emotional triggers may be the memory of a lost one that causes you to engage in this behavior that you are looking to change.

Regardless of the trigger, you can learn to not respond in the unhealthy way you have been in the past. Replace the pattern with a more acceptable behavior that will help in your goal achievement. Smokers can replace that cigarette with an after meal mint or brush their teeth after eating. You can go for a walk to unwind and distress instead of eating junk food or having a drink after work. Remember, taking small steps to achieve your higher goal is the key. As Dr. Martin Luther King Jr. said:

> "Take the first step in faith. You don't have to see the whole staircase, just take the first step."

Application

Refer back to Chapter 2 and your plan for changes.

Determine if those goals have been developed because you really want them or if someone else in your life has created this image in your mind as someone you have to be in order to be loved. What changes, if any, need to be made after reviewing your goals?

Do a little bit of research, look within yourself: Are your goals realistic?

Do they need to be adjusted or revised in any way?

What can you identify as some of your triggers?

What new behaviors can you replace the old behaviors with that will help you achieve your goal?

Rewrite some of those stinking thinking comments you make to yourself:

Here Today, Gone Tomorrow

Are there emotional issues that need to be addressed before you can make permanent changes in your life? If so, what are they? Is this something that you can change alone or do you need the support of an individual, group or therapist?

{Notes}

How to make your New Year's resolutions finally stick | Erin Bagwell

Chapter 5
Beware of Negativity

> "What we focus on, we empower and enlarge.
> Good multiplies when focused upon.
> Negativity multiplies when focused upon.
> The choice is ours: Which do we want more of?"
> ~Julia Cameron

The most important thing of which we must all be vigilant is negativity. Negativity may show up in many different forms including self-doubt, discouragement or pessimism. It permeates this world in which we live. We all have people with whom we come into contact in the workplace, in the community, and even perhaps in our families that are "negative Nelly-s" (and if you know someone named Nelly or your own name is Nelly, do not be offended… I'm sure *you* are quite positive!).

It can be quite difficult to keep a positive attitude in the mist of such a negative world. Just look around, the news is negative, doctor's reports are negative, our friends get together just to discuss all the negative things in their relationships, finances and health. There are an endless number of television shows that thrive on negativity.

I can just imagine you sitting there, reading this and thinking to yourself, "what does the world, my family, my friends, and my television being negative have to do with me losing weight, quitting smoking or [insert your goal here]?" But trust me; all of this has a lot to do with your goals!

> "A true friend never gets in your way unless you happen to be going down."
> ~Arnold H. Glasow

How to make your New Year's resolutions finally stick | Erin Bagwell

Your own personal characteristics or personality traits are most similar to the five people you spend the majority of your time with. If those five people are negative and are not able to finish things they start, it is very likely that you too are negative and do not finish things you start. If your five favorite people complain about everything, there's a good chance that you are doing it too. That may be a little hard to swallow, but it is my job to be a little in your face about things every once in a while and this is extremely important! I am only trying to help you see that it is possible to be negative simply by being exposed to negativity on a regular basis and all without even realizing it!

With that said, it is important to do a bit of self-discovery here and decide if you are a negative person or someone who tends to complain. The reason this is so important is because when you spend your time being negative, or complaining about how bad things are, your negativity brings more of that negativity into your life. You're drawing that junk to you just like a giant magnet! It may not manifest as the exact same thing you are complaining about right now, but rest assured that something to complain about will surely show up!

I know. I still didn't answer your question, did I? The reason that negativity is such a big deal when you are setting goals and working toward achieving them is because accomplishing a goal is a positive thing! If you are stuck on the Negativity Broadcasting Channel (not to be confused with the National Broadcasting Channel) you are only drawing more negativity into your life, *not* positivism (that's a weird word, but I did not make it up). Positivism means "the quality or state of being positive!" Being negative pushes that target date further and further out. If you doubt that you will be able to achieve it, you are right. You will not be able to achieve it.

> "Quit thinking that you must halt before the barrier of the inner negativity. You need not. You can crash through..."
> ~Vernon Howard

The only way to accomplish your goal is to be positive that you will achieve whatever you have set your mind to! Have no doubt in that beautiful, magnificent, wonderful, complicated, powerful brain of yours! Believe with all your heart that you will achieve you goal. Imagine yourself as already having achieved it! Do it every day! Do *not* let a seed of doubt in your mind for one moment! Believe that you will reach your goal and you *will* reach your goal. I don't care what anyone else says! *You can do it* and *you will do it*!

> "I get tired of people who don't believe in themselves."
> ~Richard Simmons

Now, when the target date is approaching and you have not made as much progress as you had hoped for, remain positive and *know* that you will do it. Do not let negativity creep in, for then negativity begins to take over.

The Vine That Ate the South

Pessimism is like a kudzu vine. I don't know how many of you know what a kudzu vine is, but if you were raised in the Southeast, you probably know exactly what I'm talking about.

History, once again is not my thing, so here is the six second version: Kudzu was brought to our country from some other country a long, long time ago. Some well-meaning soul planted it at their house here in the South thinking that it would make things oh-so-lovely. Today, the Kudzu vine is also known as the "vine that ate the South." It is *uncontrollable* and grows everywhere at an extremely fast pace, covering everything in its path. Kudzu grows approximately one foot per day. Doesn't seem like that much until you realize that every one of these vines, hundreds of thousands of these vines, are growing one foot per day! That's hundreds of thousands of feet of kudzu just taking over.

Obviously my history on the kudzu vine is not worthy of any special on the History Channel, but the point is very applicable to you in your life right now! When you are trying to become a positive thinker who sets and achieves goals effortlessly, one weak moment of negativity can creep in and swallow your optimism completely if you are not on guard.

> "Above all else, guard your heart,
> for it is the wellspring of life."
> ~Proverbs 4:23, Holy Bible,
> New International Version

When we are not on guard, this negativity can creep in very easily, especially if you already have a pattern of thinking "I can't do it." That doubtful seed may come from within yourself or even from a "naysayer" who says that your goal is impossible. These thoughts may come from people in your present, but many times they come from voices (that we play over and over) of people in our pasts.

You are trying to develop a new pattern of thinking, a positive pattern of thinking and believing, that you can do whatever you set your mind to. There will be times when others tell you that you cannot do what you are trying to do, or they will try to convince you that it is too difficult or even impossible, to do. *Do not listen to them*! Believe that it will be easy to accomplish your goal and it *will be*!

> The question isn't who is going to let me;
> it's who is going to stop me.
> ~Ayn Rand, The Fountainhead

I will not pretend to be an expert on the laws of the universe, but I do know a little about the Law of Attraction (which is exactly what we are working with here). I don't know *how* it works, but it does work! I promise. I know you might be thinking that this sounds like every other self-help book on the planet. Well, if those books were telling you to be positive and believe that you can do great things and work miracles in your own life, *they were right*! Do not discount those authors, or this book, because you have bought into the widely held idea that some things are just too hard to do.

And do not give up on thinking positively every day, about yourself and about everything in your life. Just as you need time to establish new patterns in your eating, the way you deal with stress, scheduling your time effectively, etc., you also need time to establish this new pattern of thinking. Do not give up on this idea that positive thinking makes a difference. As soon as you believe those negative kudzu-vine-thoughts that say "this stuff doesn't work," you create "not working" as your truth and all of the progress you have made goes down the toilet.

Be persistently positive. Ignore negativity and replace any hint of it with positive thoughts or statements, no matter how annoying it may seem to others around you. If you have a positive comment to say every time they have a negative comment to say, eventually they will stop trying to sell their negativity to you! And trust me, that is a good thing!

The Benefit of the Accountability Partner

Another way to help make sure that you are surrounded by encouragement and stay on track reaching your goals is to have a partner available to help you. An accountability partner can make sure you are following your steps on a daily basis, and help give you that extra bit of encouragement when you are feeling defeated. Be sure this person is encouraging and not negative!

Having another person involved helps because generally people do not like having to report to others that they have been slacking off – the potential embarrassment serves as another type of external motivation. Choose your accountability partner to be someone who has the following characteristics:

1. Someone who will be honest in their assessment of your progress on your goal;
2. Someone who will be committed to frequent communication to you;
3. Someone who is positive but firm; and
4. Someone who has a similar goal to yours (this is optional, and not a requirement for a good accountability partner).

It is not only what we do, but also what we do not do, for which we are accountable."
~Moliere

Application

Who are the 5 people you spend the most time with? Beside each name, indicate in your own way if they are positive or negative the majority of the time. You probably don't want to show this to them…

1.

2.

3.

4.

5.

Who are the 5 most positive people you have ever met?

1.

2.

3.

4.

5.

What are some things you find yourself complaining about?

Now, take a moment and write those same things in a positive manner, as if they were already exactly the way you wanted them to be. For example, if you said "my spouse and I fight all the time," write it as "my spouse and I get along all the time."

Who could be your accountability partner and what would make them a good one?

How to make your New Year's resolutions finally stick | Erin Bagwell

{Notes}

{Notes}

Chapter 6
It's Not About What You Don't Want

Most of us have the awful "habit" of proclaiming loud and clear what we do not want out of life. "I don't want to be late." "I don't want to be poor." "I don't want to be fat." "I don't want to be alone." I know this sounds familiar to you. I'd be willing to bet you talk to your friends about how you don't want things to turn out in your life. The very things you fear are the things you spend all of your time talking about at the proverbial "water cooler of life," on your breaks at work, at your children's sports practice, at the company Christmas party, and on Facebook. I used to do it. It was a bad pattern of mine. But that was before I realized the error of my ways; before I realized that talking about what I did not want actually brought those things into my life. Just like that giant magnet we talked about earlier! Now on my breaks I talk about all the ways I want my life to turn out! Trust me, it's much more uplifting, and way more fun!

> "All that we are is a result of what we have thought."
> ~Buddha

The problem with talking about what you don't want is that it tends to make those exact scenarios appear over and over again in your life. Are you afraid of being alone and never finding a partner to share your life with? You say to your friends, "Find someone for me, I'm tired of being single!" And yet, you keep on being single. Odd isn't it? It is because you are focusing on what you do *not* want instead of what you *do* want.

Resolving to change this attitude and your focus will inevitably change the other things in your life that you want to be changed. If your specific goal is to lose twenty-five pounds, talk to your friends about weighing your current weight minus that twenty-five pounds. If your specific goal is to bench press 200 pounds, talk to your family about being able to do that, *now*! Talk about it as if it were already true. Fake it 'til you make it! Imagine it. Spend time and energy visualizing your life and yourself as if you have already achieved that goal and it is already part of who you are *now*. Use your imagination!

> "All successful men and women are big dreamers. They imagine what their future could be, ideal in every respect, and then they work every day toward...that goal or purpose."
> ~Brian Tracey

I remember being a child and using my imagination for everything. We were not among the wealthiest, as a matter of fact, one of my mother's favorite stories to tell is about how she decided not to buy a sack of potatoes one week at the grocery store because she couldn't afford to spend another dollar. There is a very happy ending to that story, which I shall save for later. The point is: I didn't have a lot of fancy toys and video gaming systems to play with growing up. I had what I had, what I had been blessed with, which wasn't much but which did include my brain! And I used my brain all the time.

I imagined that my bicycle was a school bus and I was the bus driver, dropping the kids off at each driveway along my street. I imagined that the leaves, which I had so carefully raked into lines, formed the walls of a mansion. I imagined that the mud was a hamburger (which did not taste very good, might I add). I imagined that I was a teacher helping imaginary students move towards a clearer picture of reality, an understanding of the universe and themselves... I probably was really just teaching them spelling and math, but it's very similar. I'm sure you can add to this list of things you imagined when you were a child. So, why, with all this imagination we have been afforded, do we stop using it when we get to be a certain age? Your guess is as good as mine. It could be because of all the negativity we face over the years, or perhaps, because we believe that others will think we are stupid or silly if we walk around pretending all the time. But it was fun to make believe then and I'm here to tell you: it is fun *now*!

> "Imagination is everything. It is the preview of life's coming attractions."
> ~Albert Einstein

Talk about your life as though what you have imagined it to be is your current reality. Pretend you already have that brand new car! Pretend you already weigh exactly what you want to weigh. Pretend you have already stopped unhealthy habits and can run marathons. And speak to that end! "I am thin." "I am sober." "I am rich."

Oh, yes. Everyone will think you're crazy. But that's alright. And do you know why it is okay for them to think you are crazy? Because in the end you are going to have the body you want, the relationship you want, the bank account you want, the car you want… Are you beginning to get the picture? I hope so.

> "Whatever the mind can conceive, it can achieve."
> ~W. Clement Stone

Not only should you imagine how you want your life to be, but the visualization of you accomplishing your goals should create in you wonderful feelings of gratitude; gratitude that you will feel when you have achieved your goals. You need to feel thankful in advance for the strength to achieve your goals. But that's not the only gratitude you will need. You also need to feel gratitude for as much of your current life as you can *right now;* before it is accomplished. Feeling thankful for what you have now will bring your goals and dreams to you even faster. It is like putting your dreams and goals on a bullet train – zip! Before you know it, life is exactly as you have imagined it – then you can really feel those wonderful feelings of gratitude. But in the mean time, feel those feelings *now!*

> "As each day comes to us refreshed and anew, so does my gratitude renew itself daily. The breaking of the sun over the horizon is my grateful heart dawning upon a blessed world."
> ~Terri Guillemets

Application

Write a list of exactly how you want your life to be as if you are thankful for it already happening to you.

I feel so grateful now that I …

{Notes}

{Notes}

Chapter 7
Developing Your Reward System

Can I just take a moment to say that I'm proud of you! You're doing great! Learning some new things, being reminded of things you already knew. You can do it! Anyway, I digress. On we go!

Now that you have your goals established and you are talking about life as though you have already achieved those goals, it is important to develop a reward system that is specifically designed just for you. This system will work to help motivate you to achieve your goals. It is also important that this reward system work according to the time frame that you have set up for achieving those goals. Rewards are very important in our lives because they reinforce both the old behaviors that keep us alive (such as eating and breathing) and the new behaviors that we are trying to develop.

> "Whatever any man does he first must do in his mind, whose machinery is the brain. The mind can do only what the brain is equipped to do, and so man must find out what kind of brain he has before he can understand his own behavior." ~ Gay Gaer Luce and Julius Segal (From Sleep, 1966)

The brain is a very complex piece of "machinery," if you will. It has several regions that serve very unique purposes. One such region is the reward center or reward pathway, which is located in the center of the brain. This area of the brain is in charge of providing us with those feelings of drive (or motivation and inspiration), reward, and performance (or behavior). This is the "I want to" and "I think I can" center of the brain, so to speak.

To help you better understand exactly how your brain does this I will attempt to simplify a very complex subject. Basically, humans engage in a behavior that will help us increase our chance of survival (such as eating or sex for procreation), the reward pathway is activated and releases hormones, like dopamine, that make us feel good. When we feel good, this feeling increases the chances that we will engage in this behavior again, thus creating a cycle.

Eat food
Get full
Feel happy because you're
going to live another day

The reason it is so important for you to understand the way this reward center works is because in order to increase your chances of success at changing something in your life, this part of your brain needs to be activated. With the reward center activated, your chances for permanently changing the behaviors increase significantly. In order to activate the reward center, you must determine how to remove the old negative patterns that were being rewarded, either consciously or unconsciously, and replace them with new, positive behaviors along with more functional rewards.

> "If you believe in yourself and have dedication and pride - and never quit, you'll be a winner. The price of victory is high but so are the rewards."
> ~Paul Bryant

Let's use sweets for example, which is one of my old patterns that was difficult to break (and every once in a while I still have a relapse). As Gene Simmons said on one of his Family Jewels Episodes, if I was a dinosaur in my past life, "I would have been a cake-a-saurus." But I digress. The old pattern was that I would eat some type of sugary goodness and my tongue would communicate to my brain that it tasted very good. In addition to this sugary goodness tasting so yummy, my stomach was getting full at the same time, releasing dopamine (therefore telling my brain that I would not starve to death if I continued to eat things like this, perpetuating my chance for survival). Next time someone pulled a cake out of the oven or brought some doughnuts into the office, all of those wonderful, yummy memories were activated by the smell. My brain then convinced itself that eating that food would keep me alive and make me feel good. It's all part of

Here Today, Gone Tomorrow

the cycle... The reward pathway was designed to make sure that you would repeat those behaviors, whether those behaviors are good for you or not.

Unfortunately, our brain cannot tell the difference between things that are good for us that release that dopamine and things that are bad for us that release the same dopamine. That's why a runner gets a "runner's high" and a junkie gets a very different kind of high – both of these "highs" release dopamine, which feels good and both "highs" store good memories of "feeling good" in the brain hoping to keep this type of activity going.

You must begin rewarding yourself for the positive behaviors that bring you closer to your goal so that you can train your brain to release those feel-good hormones when you do the things that are helping you reach your goals. Buy yourself something nice. Go spend some time with a positive person that makes you feel wonderful about yourself. Give yourself stickers. I love to give myself stickers! What?! No one else gives them to me anymore, so why shouldn't I give them to myself?! It is part of my own personal reward system, and when I earn enough stickers, I buy myself a new pair of shoes. Now, not every time is it a new pair of shoes. Sometimes it is more of a treat, for instance a pedicure or a massage. But it doesn't have to be something that you pay for, but more about that in a moment. It doesn't matter what you're working for at first, just as long as you are working!

> "Before the reward there must be labor.
> You plant before you harvest.
> You sow in tears before you reap in joy."
> ~Ralph Ransom

It is important to keep variety in your reward system. Think of the external things that really motivate you to do a good job and use that as your reward. Eventually, the motivation should come from within yourself, but until then it is okay to use external rewards and motivation to keep yourself on track. Sometimes it takes a while for that internal motivation to take root; it must be nourished.

Also, keep in mind that not every reward means that you have to spend money. There are plenty of rewards that you can give yourself that don't require you to spend any money whatsoever. For example, take a nap, invite some friends over for a game night, take the afternoon off of work, spend time with a loved one doing something fun, or go fly a kite. Take a bubble bath or do something that makes your soul happy. If you are lucky enough to have a supportive significant other, perhaps you can have them offer you rewards, such as a back rub or a date to your favorite place.

> "Surround yourself with people who provide you with support and love and remember to give back as much as you can in return."
> ~Karen Kain

Whether you have that support network or not, you are a magnificently creative individual! Use that creativity when you are developing this reward system.

Logging your progress

It is also very important to keep track of the progress you are making. You want to be sure to record your progress every few days. I recommend that you don't go more than three days without logging some sort of entry regarding your goals. Three days will allow you to have a lazy weekend but then by Monday you should be back to the grind. And what a lovely grind it is when you are becoming a better you! There are a variety of ways that you can log this progress. Here are a few:

1. Using a day planner. You can use either the day planner you already are using at home or in the office or you can use one that is specifically for tracking your goals. Make notes throughout the day as to what you are doing to achieve your goals. Are you doing desk exercises? Are you drinking more water? How many cigarettes have you had today? How much time has it been between cigarettes? Notes about those types of things that are specifically related to your goals.

2. Using a wall calendar lets others see that you are publicly committed to reaching your goals. Write the goal for the week and then track your progress using a key or stickers! You know how fond of stickers I am.

3. Many people prefer personal journals that will allow them to have more privacy. Write your goal at the top of the page and check in every few days to log what you have done that week to reach your goal. Be cautioned though: when using a private journal, you also provide yourself with an opportunity to avoid the accountability of logging your progress in public. If you are going to use a private journal, please make sure that you also have a very strong accountability partner (which we already covered in chapter 5).

4. Check lists are also a good way to log your progress. If you break the task down into the smaller goals, then you can check off each step as it is completed. Checklists have a very satisfying way of helping encourage you to continue to make progress. This works for goals that range from writing a dissertation or book to losing two pounds per week. The only drawback is that some people find these checklists to consume more of their time than they would like. To save time, you can develop a daily checklist and make copies of it so that you have enough to log progress using those methods for a few weeks. Then change them up and make more copies.

> "The dictionary is the only place that success comes before work. Work is the key to success, and hard work can help you accomplish anything."
> ~Vince Lombardi Jr.

Regardless of which method you select to log your progress, it is important to do it. You may not like any of those suggestions I have made and decide to develop your own method of logging progress. That's wonderful. You don't have to use one of these four methods to record progress, there are many other ways. But the important thing is that you are recording it. When you have a bad day or feel discouraged, take a look back at how far you have come (even if it has only been a week) and feel encouraged! *You are making progress!!!*

Logging your progress does take additional time. Prepare for the time it will take up front. Then commit to it. Logging your progress is crucial in actually making forward motion on your goals. Some people find it annoying to actually have to count calories or track other progress but it is suggested so often because it helps you be consciously aware of what you are doing, or not doing, in working towards your goals. Progress requires work. Not just a dream.

Application

What are some things that you can begin using as rewards for yourself? Try to list at least 10.

What are some of the ways you have rewarded yourself for negative or dysfunctional behaviors in the past?

Take time to write out one or two of the short term goals and what reward you will receive once those are achieved (remember to include a time frame):

Take a moment to develop your plan for tracking your progress:

{Notes}

{Notes}

Chapter 8
Sharing Your Goals with Others

> "We have all a better guide in ourselves, if we would attend to it, than any other person can be."
> ~ Jane Austen

I'm sure you can think of at least a few people with whom you would like to share these new goals. You may even want to share them with everyone you run into at home, work and even a stranger or two. A word of caution: remember that when you are trying to achieve your goals it is very important to surround yourself with positive "you can do it" attitudes, both from yourself and from those around you.

You might not even want to tell those people that you know are negative (remember the "negative Nelly's" we talked about earlier) about your goal. As a general rule: unless the person you are telling about your goal is going to support you 100%, it is none of their business.

> "When you jump for joy, beware that no one moves the ground from beneath your feet."
> ~Stanislaw Lee

There are many ways you can share your goal with others. And even more now that we have the privilege of living in such a technologically savvy society. Here are some suggestions that you may want to consider when sharing your goals:

1. Verbally tell those positive people who uplift and encourage you about your goals.

2. Post it on a social network, like Facebook or Twitter – I have found that the negative people generally don't respond to positive electronic postings. If they don't think you can do it, they tend to keep it to themselves. I mean, imagine how it would look if you have

800 "likes" on Facebook and seventy-two "you can do it" comments and that one negative person gets on there and says "I don't think it's possible." They are probably going to have 872 comments back to them about how being so negative is such an awful thing to do to someone who is working so hard to achieve a goal. So in this sense, you've got a whole network of people who've got your back!

3. Make a vision board – cut out pictures, draw pictures, find visual images representing what it is that you want to accomplish and put them all together on a "vision board." Sit and look at that board daily and envision yourself accomplishing the goal. This should be done daily for the best results – imagination actually moves into reality through your visualization. Have fun with this, it should never feel like a chore. Imagine how it will feel when your goal is realized. Feel all the good feelings and the gratitude.

4. Post reminders of your goal in the places that you visit often – the kitchen, the bathroom (I even put one in the bathroom at work, which everyone else thought was very funny), your office, your bedroom, the sun visor in your car, wherever you can think of that you visit or see frequently. When posting the reminders make sure you write it in a way that reflects yourself already having reached the goal.

5. Tell people about your progress – there is nothing wrong with bragging on yourself every now and then. Don't try to make others jealous or feel badly about themselves, but encourage them that if you can do it so can they!

6. Log your progress (as we discussed in chapter 7). A day by day planner can be very helpful in recording all the things you have done that day to either get you closer to your goal or further away from your goal. A daily planner is also helpful in the sense that you will be able to use that after one month to look back and see how far you have come. This will also help you to focus on the progress you have made, not just the journey that remains ahead of you.

Here Today, Gone Tomorrow

How to make your New Year's resolutions finally stick | Erin Bagwell

Application

List some more ways you can share your goals with positive and encouraging people in your life:

Which of the methods that I mention seem to be the best suited for your personality? Or can you think of another method that may work better for you?

List at least 5 places you can post reminders to yourself:

{Notes}

{Notes}

Chapter 9
Flexibility Is Not Just for Muscles

It is important to remember that the goals you set for yourself should not be inflexible, unmoving, non-negotiable contracts. When you do not allow yourself to be flexible with your goals, they turn from positive agents of change into negative roadblocks that make you feel worse about yourself. *So what* if you do not accomplish your goal exactly on schedule? Is it the end of the world? Absolutely not! Does this mean the goal should be thrown out with the garbage? Um, let me think about this, *no*! Should you just give up? *Are you crazy*?! Although schedules are an important part of accomplishing goals, sometimes life throws us curve balls. Sometimes the very business of living can get in the way of our best laid plans. Sometimes this is a good thing, sometimes it is not.

> "Don't worry if you don't complete everything on the schedule. At least you will have completed the most important projects before getting to the less important ones."
> ~Ivy Lee

While I was in graduate school, I had come to a particularly difficult juncture. I had become very discouraged. At that point in my graduate career, which was a part time program taking about five years to complete, many of us were very discouraged because it seemed that the light at the end of the tunnel (our graduation) would never arrive. I was very dejected. I had been working so hard at a job that I absolutely hated, plus spending countless hours on my school work. I could not see an end in sight. I was tired and out of steam. I didn't feel like pushing onward, or fighting the good fight anymore. It was at this time in my graduate career, one of my professors told me, "Sometimes life gets in the way of education."

And life certainly did get in the way of my education. I decided to get married and to take a semester off from graduate school. This was a very hectic semester. The wedding was in December, right before finals and then the semester following (the one that I took off from school) was spent heading speedily towards a divorce. In this case, life interfered with my education.

Over the years, I have learned that life can interfere with more than just your plan to graduate. Life tends to be non-biased in the interruptions with which it deals us. Some of these interruptions can quickly be seen as a blessing, some are perceived to be more negative.

Vacations get in the way of weight loss. Work-related stressors overwhelm and make it nearly impossible to stop smoking. Weather prohibits outdoor activities. Illness interferes with productivity at work, hampering that raise. A death in the family makes it difficult to attend personal growth meetings you have scheduled for yourself. The list could include anything that the business of life covers, but I feel like you understand my point.

Just as I have experienced in my life, in your life there have been times when goals were not accomplished by your deadline because of unpredictable circumstances. Sometimes, the only thing that you *can* predict about life is the way you are going to respond to those unpredictable situations. You cannot control how others respond; you can only control how you respond. Within your response to those curve balls of life lies your *power*.

> "The power inside you is energy amplified."
> ~Claire Todae

When you fall off the wagon, you have the power to get up all over again, dust yourself off and hop, climb or drag yourself back onto that wagon. Knowing that you just have to do it, that *you can* do it and then getting it done – no ifs, ands or buts about it – is your power! It is that "I have to have it" attitude. You must believe in yourself. For if you do not believe in yourself, who else then can believe in you? And, you must decide now that even if your schedule gets crazy at work for a few weeks, or there is some type of emergency in the family that derails you for a while, you *will* continue your journey and you *will* achieve your goals.

Here Today, Gone Tomorrow

> "Stay committed to your decisions, but
> stay flexible in your approach."
> ~Tom Robbins

Being flexible will allow you to pick yourself up and carry on. Remember to look how far you have come on your journey before you begin to berate yourself. When we berate ourselves, or engage in thinking that tears us down and lowers our self-esteem or our confidence in our ability to achieve our goals, it is then that we begin that downward spiral. It takes much less time to destroy your new positive pattern of living than it does to establish it. And as you slip further and further into that "stinking thinking" the chances that you are going to give up completely grow more and more! Even if you have only been working on your goal for one day, you are moving forward, which is something to be celebrated! Make it a point to record the small steps so that you can look back and see where you have been and encourage yourself to continue on your journey as soon as life allows you to do so again.

I must take this time to say that there is a difference between a legitimate interference and an interference that we allow to be larger than it really is. Sometimes we exaggerate the interference so that we feel justified in giving up on our goals. Do not use life as an excuse to not achieve your goals! Life is going to happen. But do not be derailed by the small things. Focus and be disciplined.

> "The only discipline that lasts is self-discipline."
> ~Bum Philips

Feelers and Doers

In my brief life on this earth, I have observed that there are two types of people in the world: feelers and doers. A feeler, which is the kind of person I used to identify myself as, will only do things when he or she *feels* like doing them. If he doesn't feel good one day, he will not do what he needs to do, regardless of how important it may be that he do it. Feelers are governed by their emotions and usually wait for inspiration to strike before they take any action. Now, every once in a while I allow myself to let the feeling part of my personality govern me, however, this is not the side of me that needs to be operating when I am trying to accomplish my goals. This is the side of me that is best utilized in other areas of my life.

Doers are those that do what they have to do *regardless* of how they feel that day. They are governed by logic and self-discipline. They may feel like staying in bed but they also know that going for the morning jog is what they need to do to start their day off right and achieve their goal. Though each type of person has strengths and weaknesses, it is important to develop a "doer attitude" when working on goal achievement. Nike had it right when they coined the phrase "Just Do It."

> "The world needs dreamers and the world needs doers. But above all, the world needs dreamers who do."
> ~Sarah Ban Breathnach

If it is self-discipline you desire, you must adopt the belief that you will complete whatever task has to be done regardless of what obstacles or feelings get in the way of accomplishing it. Now, that does not mean that if you are bed-ridden because of pneumonia that you should still get up and run a marathon. But it does mean that you can use the power within yourself to improve your health, and circumstances, in order to start working towards your goals once again.

The most powerful people in the world will tell you that deep within them existed a need to accomplish their goals so badly, they felt as though they would *perish* if they did not accomplish the goal. Perish, die, expire, pass away, or depart from this life… (Thank you thesaurus!) This is the "I have to have it" attitude I keep mentioning. This is an extremely powerful motivating force. This is the same attitude that you need to have when working towards becoming the "best you" you can be. Think to yourself: "I must achieve this goal to survive, to grow, to prosper…to survive." And work towards that goal with unbridled ambition, passion and determination.

"It is not necessary to change.
Survival is not mandatory."
~W. Edwards Deming

Application

Reflect on the following quote:

"Inspiration seldom generates action.
Action always generates inspiration."
~Unknown

{Notes}

{Notes}

Here Today, Gone Tomorrow

Chapter 10
Slow and Steady Wins the Race

*"Let thy step be slow and steady,
that thou stumble not."
~Ieyasu Tokugawa*

Remember the age-old tale about the tortoise and the hare? It was reported to be the race of the century! The gun sounded and they were off! The hare shot out of the gate and was favored to win by a huge margin. But, you know as well as I do that he didn't finish triumphantly, now did he? No! The tortoise, with odds stacked against him, and, naturally, a much slower competitor than the quick-paced hare, kept moving steadily toward the finish line for the win! The message of this fable is the lesson of this chapter: "Slow and steady wins the race."

In our society, we have heard this saying over and over again. We have taught it to our children, but for some reason we maintain that inpatient attitude, similar to a toddler in the throes of the terrible twos. "Patience is a virtue," we teach the little ones, but we rarely listen to this advice ourselves.

To reach the goals you have set for yourself, you need to adjust your mind-set from the hare's ("quick, fast and in a hurry") to that of the tortoise ("I will get there, I must keep working as hard as my mind and body can work"). You have got to throw that "all or nothing" mentality in the garbage. It is not serving you as much as you think it is.

You need to ease yourself into this change – not forgoing your passion and purpose. Starting your journey towards change with superhuman resolve inevitably leads to a terrible tumble off of the proverbial wagon and, eventually, to the place where you surrender the belief in yourself that you *can* change.

Approaching goals with this all-or-nothing method is very appealing, and can even be motivating at times, but overreaching those bounds is the most hazardous way to come out of the gate. Some personalities do thrive on this principal but I have found that the majority of us do not. Human beings are imperfect. Believe it or not, we *learn* to be that way as our lives move forward. For those of you wanting to lose weight: when you *do* skip a workout or give in to temptation (something we all do), you are more likely to throw in the towel if you have the belief that you must change everything all at once.

> "I change too quickly: my today refutes my yesterday. When I ascend I often jump over steps, and no step forgives me that."
> ~Friedrich Nietzsche

Other Morals from the Tortoise

Slow and steady is not the only moral to be learned from this story. Of course the hare was the faster of the two animals; however, he should not have *assumed* that he could win the race without any *effort* on his part. In our fast-food society, we have a tendency to assume that things should be easy and immediate. Everyone is looking for the quick fix, a magic pill solution to their problems. We often forget that living can require hard work at times.

We are so accustomed to being able to get food from the grocery store, forgetting that somewhere, someone had to toil to harvest that food and then deliver it to the place where we can easily select what we want. The farmer plants his harvest and then patiently waits for it to surrender what he has sown. And he reaps exactly what he has sown. Not more. Many times, less than he has sown. We can no longer buy into the idea that we get bigger or more extravagant results than what we have invested into our harvest.

The hare was foolish to believe that he could reap a win without sowing the effort. I am cautioning you to understand that you will reap from your efforts that which you put in. Not more. Your results will mirror your efforts to achieve those results. If you expect to make lasting change in your life, you must consciously act and behave in a manner that is consistent with the results you desire.

> "Your heart is full of fertile seeds, wanting to sprout. Just as a lotus flower s prings from the mire to bloom splendidly, the interaction of the cosmic breath causes the flower of the spirit to bloom and bear fruit in this world."
> ~Morihei Ueshiba

In order to set yourself up for success, you need to start thinking like that tortoise. Pace yourself. Reward yourself for your progress, take a day off now and then, but don't stray too far from the path that will lead you to your goals. Behave in a manner that will produce the results you are looking for. Hold tight to patience, self-discipline and the morals we teach our children through fables like The Tortoise and the Hare. Give yourself a break every once in a while, and I don't just mean a break from your plan to achieve your goal. I mean a mental break. Don't be so hard on yourself. And when you make a mistake, which is bound to happen, keep going! You would never teach your children to give up after making a mistake on something they were trying to do for the very first time. Or even for the 100th time!

> "You'll make [mistakes], but so what? That's why they're called mis-takes. Humor relaxes the uptight ego. You get a new cue from your inner Self and simply say, "I missed my cue, so let's do a second take." Your willingness to take the risk of making a mistake is actually an expression of courage and a willingness to grow from them. Mistakes are about getting the blessing in the lesson and the lesson in the blessing."
> ~Michael Bernard Beckwith

This may not be your first crack at working towards this goal, but it may be the first time you are trying to achieve it using these methods. Maybe it's not the first time. Maybe you have forgotten what you have learned in the past. Maybe you weren't in the place then to accomplish what you can accomplish now. It's a new day. You're a different you already, just from the experience of living. Have patience and discipline, and trust the process. You will change! And in the mean time, those whom you love, including your children may learn a thing or two about how to successfully set goals and discipline themselves in a way that makes those goals achievable.

> "Present yourself always
> As who you would be,
> And this person
> The world will see."
> ~Robert Brault

Application

Think of some other morals we teach children. Many of these we often forget to apply to ourselves. What are some of the morals or fables that come to mind and what lessons can you use from them?

{Notes}

{Notes}

Chapter 11
The Bottom Line

> "Man is never alone. Acknowledged or unacknowledged, that which dreams through him is always there to support him from within."
> ~Laurence van der Post

You have been given a lot of information in the past ten chapters. Is it making sense to you? I sure hope so! The bottom line is that goals provide direction for our lives. Research shows that people who regularly set and reach goals live longer because they have something in life to look forward to! Goals help bring a focus to our lives so that we can live out our dreams — no matter how big or how small they may be. We are all born with a desire to grow towards the most ideal version of ourselves; to evolve. Take the acorn for instance. Within the acorn lies the potential to become a magnificent oak tree. It only needs to be nurtured with soil, water and sunlight. We are like spiritual acorns, longing to grow into our magnificence. Goals help us to do that very thing. It is natural for you to have that desire to grow towards a better, upgraded version of yourself. Embrace that desire.

Embrace that desire with the understanding that within you lies a powerful force that has been stunted over the years. Too many unsuccessful attempts at change have inhibited that power, your power. This concept is what we refer to as "learned helplessness." The baby elephant is tethered to a spike in the ground and despite his bravest attempts to free himself; he is not strong enough to do so. And so, when he becomes a full grown adult elephant, with exponentially more strength, he does not even *attempt* to break the tether and escape, for he has learned that he is not strong enough and believes that he cannot free himself, therefore he remains a prisoner.

> "Learned helplessness is the giving-up reaction, the quitting response that follows from the belief that whatever you do doesn't matter."
> ~Arnold Schwarzenegger

For some of you this innate desire to evolve may be completely dormant, for others it may only be partially bruised. But that powerful force within you is the ability to achieve the ideal version of yourself. Quantum physics has proven that your mind is literally broadcasting signals into the universe on a *measurable* frequency that attracts similar things back to you. You are always creating, always manifesting, in your life what you are focusing on. If you focus your energy, the power of your mind, your determination and your intention on achieving your goals, you *cannot* fail!

> "How we spend our days
> is how we spend our lives."
> ~Annie Dillard

The person that you are when the curtain is drawn and the audience has gone is the person that really matters. That is your character: who you are when no one else is around. Do you have the type of character that you value most in others? Do you have the qualities in yourself that you find important and appealing in others? Goals help us develop those characteristics that we find appealing in others.

> "There are no shortcuts to
> any place worth going."
> ~Beverly Sills

Goals help you become the person you want to be, and help you to have the kind of life you want. Setting and achieving goals help you to experience the health, happiness and prosperity you are longing for. There is no magic wand that I could give to you. I cannot make it any easier for you than what has been laid out in the preceding chapters -- change is never easy. Sheer determination, a strong will and that longing within you to achieve those goals is what will bring them to fruition and make them a reality instead of a dream.

Without passion behind your purpose, you have no power to attain your goals. If you want to reach your goal, you must sincerely want to make those changes. If you are content where you are, living the life you are living, wearing the size you are wearing, why would you even bother reading a book like this? Perhaps, it is because society gave you the impression that there was something about yourself that you needed to change. But I don't believe that is what has urged you to pick up this book. I believe that you truly do have the passion and purpose to work towards achieving your goals!

You have the tools. You have the information. You know more about goal setting than the average Joe. I have done my part in providing you with the best information I could. Now, I pass the torch to you. It is your job at this moment to take that information and run with it. Not at a breakneck speed like our friend the hare, but at a slow and steady pace that will make lasting changes to your patterns, your schedule, your life and your character.

> "We did not change as we grew older;
> we just became more clearly ourselves."
> ~Lynn Hall

Take a moment to imagine that with me right now! You! Achieving your goal! How does it feel to have that raise? How does it feel to weigh the perfect weight? How does it feel to run a marathon? It feels wonderful! Enjoy those feelings of power, those "I did it!" feelings! No one can ever take those feelings away from you! Not even now, even though you are just beginning your journey. Hold on to those feelings of accomplishment and pride. Use those as fuel to propel you towards the *you* that you want to become!

I am so excited for you to complete your journey. I am so excited that you are reaching your potential and fulfilling your dreams! I know you can do it! I leave you with the following in hopes that all your wildest dreams come true and this life becomes the magnificent life you were meant to experience!

Irish Blessing

May the road rise up to meet you.
May the wind be always at your back.
May the sun shine warm upon your face;
the rains fall soft upon your fields and until we
meet again, may God hold you in the
palm of His hand.

Endnotes

Chapter 3

The adapted list that is found in the application section of this chapter is adapted from John C. Norcross and James D Guy, Jr.'s book, *Leaving it at the Office (2007)*. The information is originally designed to be part of a Therapist's Self-Care Checklist to ensure that those in the helping profession are helping themselves, however I find that parts of it are very applicable to everyone's life.

How to make your New Year's resolutions finally stick | Erin Bagwell

www.ingramcontent.com/pod-product-compliance
Lightning Source LLC
Chambersburg PA
CBHW040300170426
43193CB00020B/2961